GETTING TO KNOW

Java

DON RAUF

rosen publishing's
rosen central®

New York

Published in 2019 by The Rosen Publishing Group, Inc.
29 East 21st Street, New York, NY 10010

Library of Congress Cataloging-in-Publication Data

Names: Rauf, Don, author.
Title: Getting to know Java / Don Rauf.
Description: First edition. | New York : Rosen Publishing, 2019. | Series: Code power : a teen programmer's guide | Includes bibliographical references and index. | Audience: Grades 5–8.
Identifiers: LCCN 2018008359| ISBN 9781508183723 (library bound) | ISBN 9781508183747 (pbk.)
Subjects: LCSH: Java (Computer program language)—Juvenile literature.
Classification: LCC QA76.73.J38 R37 2019 | DDC 005.13/3—dc23
LC record available at https://lccn.loc.gov/2018008359

Manufactured in the United States of America

{ CONTENTS

```
$menuclass = 'horiznav';
$topmenuclass ='top_menu'
```

W hen it comes to computer programming languages, Java is hot. According to the TIOBE Index for 2018, which measures the use of programming languages, Java is currently more popular than several widely used languages, including C++, Python, C#, PHP, and JavaScript. Java runs the applications on Android smartphones, builds video games, and operates many web functions. To one degree or another, Java has been the tool behind the construction of many popular websites, including LinkedIn, eBay, Amazon, and Google. In addition, billions of devices hum along on Java, from ATMs to parking meters to Blu-ray players. Surprisingly, however, Java is not used to program the coffee makers that pump out hot java. Typically, these run on the languages C or C++.

While C and C++, both invented in the 1970s, are still popular today, Java surpassed them when James Gosling invented it in 1991. He created the language at Sun Microsystems in California while working with a small group of engineers called the Green Team. Today, all materials related to Java come from

>> James Gosling, shown here, is one of the most respected members of the computer science community because of his work developing Java.

the computer technology company Oracle, which bought Sun Microsystems in 2010.

The roots of Java can be found in a program called Oak, named after a tree that stood outside an engineer's office. Originally, Gosling and the Green Team developed the Oak program to operate an interactive, handheld home-entertainment controller that was targeted at the digital cable television industry. By 1994, the program had evolved into Java. The name changed along the way because it turned out another company, Oak Technology, was already using it. In an interview in JavaWorld.com, Kim Polese, who was the Oak product manager, said she named the program Java because it "reflected the essence of the technology: dynamic, revolutionary, lively, fun."

>> In 2010, Java got a new home when Oracle—a large computer technology company—purchased Sun Microsystems.

Gosling and the Green Team succeeded in making a language that was simple, secure (it can be used to write tamper-free and virus-protected systems), and operated on multiple operating systems. Java's catchphrase was "write once, run anywhere." Code written on one computer in this new lingo could run on another computer system. Gosling and colleagues concocted a system that eliminated some of the tedious aspects of writing code. Java allowed the user to write bits of code that could be reused later without needing to rewrite the code over and over again. As internet use became widespread in the 1990s, the designers realized that the new language was ideal for creating online applications. In 1995, the team announced that the Netscape Navigator internet browser would incorporate Java technology. Navigator became the dominant web browser in the 1990s. Popular browsers of today, such as Safari, Explorer, Firefox, and Chrome, also support Java applications.

Although it is now more than twenty years old, Java remains highly in demand. Plus, many consider it relatively simple to learn compared to other programming languages. In an interview with TechRepublic, James Milligan, director of digital technology at the recruiting firm Hays, said, "You can grasp the basics through an online course." Java is considered a good foundation for learning other programming languages as well. So for those interested in exploring coding, getting a taste of Java is highly recommended.

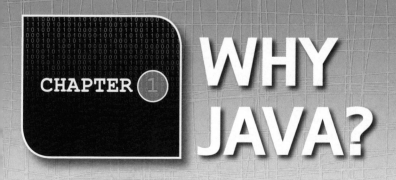

CHAPTER ① WHY JAVA?

Java is one of the most popular programming languages in the world, operating on more than seven billion devices and used by more than nine million developers around the globe. Airplane systems, ATMs, cell phones, computers, medical equipment, and televisions all run on Java. Java has also become the language of Android mobile app development. Kickstarter and WordPress apps are created with Java, as are the VLC media player, MovieGuide, the music apps Timber and Phonograph, the games *Pixel Dungeon*, *Brothers in Arms, and Free Flight Sim: 3D Airplane Simulator*. There are Java-based Google apps for YouTube video downloads, Facebook Messenger, Instagram, Netflix, Spotify, and Uber.

For those interested in coding today, knowledge of Java is a must. Many technology professionals consider it easy to learn, with a coding style that has been called almost intuitive (meaning it comes naturally).

For those interested in learning, experimenting, and constructing with Java, it is free and open-source software. "Open source" means the source code is made freely available and may be redistributed and modified. Open-source software

>> Android, which takes full advantage of Java's capabilities, runs on more than two billion mobile devices across the globe.

gives developers more freedom to create and share their work. The general public can access it freely today at the Oracle website. A downloadable Java Development Kit provides all one needs for building applications and components using the Java programming language.

THE MIND IN THE MACHINE

Electronic devices and systems don't operate on their own. Many depend on the electronic "brainpower" provided by a computer chip within. Called an embedded processor or a logic chip, this microprocessor tells a machine how to function. ATMs, for example, rely on processors to receive instructions from users so they can perform the tasks required—accept deposits, make withdrawals, issue balance statements, etc. Basically, the ATM is a data terminal, and its embedded processor communicates with the bank's host processor, which holds the actual details about customer bank accounts. The host processor checks the details submitted by the cardholder (including the security code); if everything checks out, the transaction is completed.

When it comes to websites, Java is known for its server-side powers. Many major companies that need to handle a large volume of traffic—such as Sam's Club, Amazon, and the Apple App Store—depend on it. Twitter, which supports more than four

>> Amazon and Twitter, two of the internet's biggest websites, use Java for their servers, which have to process immense amounts of data every day.

hundred million tweets a day, has its core infrastructure based on a Java system. Java programming performs all the work on a company's server, which is a computer designed to process requests and deliver data to other computers over the internet or a local network. The server side, also called the back end, houses web pages that can be accessed over the internet by clients through their web browsers. The Java programming tells a website or application how to behave.

The client side, also called the front end, refers to the web browser. Client-side codes (which are largely written in Javascript) run on someone's personal computer after a web page is loaded.

AN OBJECT-ORIENTED STYLE

There are different styles or ways of programming, called paradigms. Programmers use different paradigms to organize software so it works as desired. One common style of programming is called procedural. This paradigm uses a list of tasks that gives the computer step-by-step instructions. Most of the original programming languages are procedural, including C, COBOL, and Fortran.

Java, on the other hand, is an object-oriented programming (OOP) language. OOP languages think of data as objects and use a collection of interacting objects instead of a long list of commands. Each of these objects performs a distinct role. An object in an animation program, for example, may tell a character to walk or jump. An object will also know how to interact with other objects in the program.

Any object-oriented language—including Java—uses classes. A class is the code that is the blueprint for the object and describes its contents. The class describes data fields and defines operations, called methods. By sending a message to an object, it executes one of its methods.

OOP is often used when there is a lot of code that can be shared and reused. When an object is created to handle a complex task or behavior, a programmer can easily use that object again anywhere in his or her code. Procedural code can be easy to follow, but it gets difficult to maintain when there are huge amounts of code.

Because objects are reusable, OOP increases speed and efficiency, and Java in particular has been shown to outperform other languages in terms of speed. Developers often use it because it eases some of the workload when writing software.

>>JAVASCRIPT AND JAVA ARE DIFFERENT ANIMALS

Because of the names of these two common computer-programming languages, people sometimes think that Java and JavaScript are related. JavaScript, however, is not part of the Java platform. While they are both object-oriented languages, they are very different. As the developer Jeremy Keith said in 2009, "Java is to JavaScript as ham is to hamster." Here are a few differences.

JavaScript is typically used to make interactive effects within web browsers. Java's applets, which also did this, are declining in popularity. While Java is known as a workhorse for servers, JavaScript code has traditionally run on browsers only—although it has been gaining ground for server programming. Java code needs to be compiled, while JavaScript code is all in text. Overall, JavaScript is considered less complex than Java, and it is a great language to learn if someone wants to make lively, interactive web pages.

So why do they have similar names if they are so different? JavaScript was originally developed by Brendan Eich of Netscape under the name Mocha, which was later renamed to LiveScript. In 1995, Netscape and Sun Microsystems made a licensing agreement and the language was renamed JavaScript. It was intended to compliment Java as a scripting language (meaning it did not have to be compiled). At the time, Java was a hot new programming language, and some believed that the naming of JavaScript was intended to give the product more prestige and buzz.

>> Brendan Eich, shown here, developed JavaScript in the 1990s to work alongside Java for advanced applications and users.

THE FULL JAVA WORKS

When one considers Java, it goes beyond just the language. It includes the whole Java platform, which is the entire environment that supports the language and the building of web systems and applications. This includes its compiler, Java's Virtual Machine (JVM), libraries, frameworks, and application programming interfaces (APIs). The Java Runtime Environment (JRE) is a bundle developed and offered by Oracle, which includes the Java Virtual Machine (JVM), libraries, and other components necessary to run Java applications and applets (small applications that perform specific tasks).

When someone downloads Java software, he or she receives this runtime environment, which gives that person everything he or she needs to run Java on a web browser. The JRE includes Java plug-in software that allows applets written in the Java programming language to run inside various browsers. Web developers have used applets to bring functionality to a web page—creating interactive buttons, check boxes, forms, and other small animations on web pages. Today, the applet is almost dead, replaced by other technology—JRE 9 continues to provide the Java plug-in and support launching applets on browsers that still offer standard plug-in support but is available only for limited use and not recommended, according to Oracle.

TRANSLATING TOOLS

Like many computer languages, the Java platform has tools—a compiler and interpreter—that translate the language so machines can understand it. A compiler is a special program that transforms statements written in one programming language into a code that a computer's processor will eventually use. This platform-independent language is called Java bytecode. Although bytecode is similar to machine language, it is not the machine language of any actual computer. The Java compiler also tells a user when he or she has made a mistake using Java's "grammar," or syntax. Dr. Bill McCarty, the coauthor of *Object-Oriented Programming in Java*, compares the compiler to a stern taskmaster who "tolerates absolutely no departure from the official rules of the Java language." It is important to pick up these syntax errors early in development rather than later, when a product may have been shipped out to the public.

>> Despite constant hardware and software wars between huge companies, such as Microsoft and Apple, Java is known for being able to work on countless devices.

Java's Virtual Machine is the interpreter. The JVM deciphers the bytecode that has been produced by the compiler. All computers operate in different ways, and the JVM translates the Java bytecode into executable instructions. A computer system with the JVM installed can run Java programs regardless of the computer system on which the applications were originally developed. Each type of computer needs its own Java bytecode interpreter, but all these interpreters interpret the same bytecode language.

Oracle explains that because of the JVM, a Java program developed on a personal computer (PC) with the Windows NT operating system (OS) should run equally well without modification on a Sun Ultra workstation with the Solaris operating system, and vice versa.

Another part of the platform is APIs. These are time-saving, ready-made libraries of compiled code to use in Java programs. Frameworks consist of multiple libraries. They are large bodies of prewritten code that anyone can add to their own code to save time.

UNDERSTANDING JAVA BASICS

inus Torvalds, a software engineer who developed technology behind Linux operating systems, Android, and Chrome OS, once said, "Most good programmers do programming not because they expect to get paid or get adulation by the public, but because it is fun to program." In theory, programming should be fun and creative—and it often is. But if someone is a total newbie to the programming game, learning a computer language like Java takes some time. Thinking in code is a very unique process. It can take up to six months to learn the basics and two to three years to become fairly proficient. The process depends on many factors—time put in, learning ability, and natural talent.

THE PLUSES AND MINUSES

When it comes to Java, the language gets mixed reviews. Some think Java is clunky and requires more work than other languages. One Java user online said that Java is about as much fun as watching beige paint dry on the wall of a shuttered DMV office. Critics have called it verbose, requiring too much work to get things running properly.

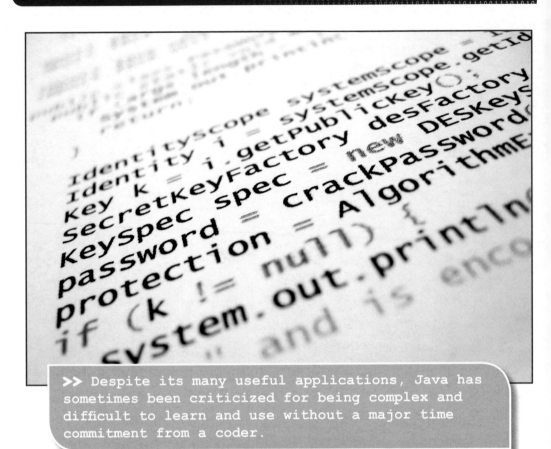

>> Despite its many useful applications, Java has sometimes been criticized for being complex and difficult to learn and use without a major time commitment from a coder.

Fans of Java, however, find it very beginner friendly because it has a syntax (or structure) that is intuitive. It can be easy to write, read, and understand. Some languages, such as C++, are more complex than Java, although Java uses a syntax that is similar to C++. If someone learning Java has any experience with that language, it can be helpful.

Java has a toolset and editors that let users know right away if they have made any mistakes. And there is a vast community of Java users that can be tapped into online for any questions or problems.

>> A part of everyday life for billions of people as well as multinational business interests, computer technology is the engine behind countless smartphones, servers, and other devices.

COMPUTING FUNDAMENTALS

For those with little or no knowledge, the journey to mastering Java starts with gaining a fundamental understanding of how computers and programming works in general. Before someone even attempts to write a single line of code, he or she has to grasp some essentials.

Computer programming requires an interest in problem solving. It involves creativity, logic, and patience. Patience is especially key because it can take time to fully understand the structure of code and how that code can tell computers what they need to do. Sometimes, the work may seem overwhelming, so it helps to take a pause and a deep breath and get the help needed to understand each step in the learning process. Without code and computers, the entire modern world as humankind knows it would collapse. It may be difficult to learn, but it is incredibly important!

Computers have four main functions involved with handling information. They take in information from the user; they manipulate that information; they store information; and they output information.

A BINARY BRAIN

On a certain level, everything in a computer operates off a binary system. In everyday life, most humans use the decimal system. This system is based on the numerals 1 through 9 and 0. A binary system, on the other hand, uses just 0s and 1s to represent numbers, letters, and other data.

Today's computers operate with transistors. Computers contain millions or billions of these transistors. They are tiny switches that trigger electric signals. Transistors are the building blocks for computer chips, which make up processing and memory units. As a collection of switches, transistors can either be on or off. Computers operate from combinations of transistors being turned on or off. Binary code is the language that tells the computer which switches to turn on (with a 1) and which switches to turn off (with a 0).

It would be almost impossible to write code with billions of 1s and 0s, so computer scientists figured out how to write coding languages that are much simpler. When a program is written

>> No matter what programming language someone uses, a computer can really only understand 1s and 0s. This binary is also known as machine code, as it can be read by machines.

in a language like Java and is ready to run, it is put through a compiler that converts the instructions into a machine code that can be read and executed by a computer. Machine code is the elemental language of 1s and 0s that tells the computer what to do.

PUTTING OBJECTS TOGETHER

Because Java handles large programs, it was developed as an object-oriented language. Basically, the objects in Java are predeveloped pieces of code. Programmers that use this type of code do not necessarily need to see the code that makes up the actual "object." They know how to fit the objects together to build their programs.

An object can have multiple variables (called attributes or properties) for storing different types of data, and it can have its own particular functions (called methods) to manipulate the object's variables. These terms can be difficult to understand at first, but the more someone works with programming, the clearer they will become.

TAKING THE FIRST STEP

Before a user can write and run a simple Java program, he or she needs to install the platform on his or her computer system. It is possible to download the Java Software Development Kit free of charge for Linux, Windows, Mac, and Solaris operating systems at Oracle.com. Once the Java platform is installed and configured for their systems, users can try to write and run a very simple program.

Many lessons in coding begin with teaching the "Hello, World!" program. This is a program that simply prints the words "Hello, World!" to the screen. Typically, a program will be written in a text editor, which is a tool provided with operating systems and software development packages. Text editors are used to

JAVA Programming

```java
public class HelloWorld {
    public static void main (String[] args) {
        System.out.println("Hello, World");
    }
}
```

>> For decades, a "Hello, World!" program has been the first step taken for countless beginner coders who are interested in learning a programming langauge—including Java.

enter programming language source statements. This program should be saved as HelloWorld.java. Then, users access the code by that name later and run it on their computers.

This simple code for a "Hello, World!" program is written like this:

```
public class Main {
    public static void main(String[] args) {
        System.out.println("Hello, World!");   } }
```

The first line of the code declares that it is public, meaning it has public access. Any other class can access it.

The second line in the application is called the main method. Every application in Java must contain a main method. The Java compiler starts to execute the code from the main method. This line is a mandatory line of code that serves as a main entry point for the program to run. Understanding each piece of the code requires more in-depth study. For example, String[] args means that a person can see and edit "arguments." Arguments are independent items, or variables, that contain data or codes.

The last line of the code is really the meat of the program, and it tells the computer what to do. "Println" is telling your computer to write the string (which is the provided text) "Hello, World!" on the computer screen and then insert a line break.

This simple bit of code gives beginners some idea of how the Java computer language works, but understanding all the bits and pieces demands some intensive learning. According to the Java syntax, each statement must end in a semicolon and a single line comment must begin with two forward slashes. Methods and classes are defined with curly braces.

>>DIG IN DEEPER: ONLINE TUTORIALS

To learn more about programming in Java, new users can explore the many resources that are available on the internet. Here are a few well-established websites to explore:

Code Academy: Since 2011, CodeAcademy.com has provided free interactive coding classes for different programming languages, including Java. The site charges for some additional services.

(continued on the next page)

>> Online coding and computer science courses, such as those hosted on Udemy, can be a major help for beginners who are feeling overwhelmed.

(continued from the previous page)

LearnJavaOnline.org: This free interactive tutorial is designed for all levels of programmers—from the absolute beginners to the more experienced.

Udemy: Launched in 2009, Udemy.com has offered more than sixty-five thousand online courses. Hundreds of thousands of students have takes its Java Tutorial for Complete Beginners, which is designed for those who have no prior programming knowledge.

Youth Digital: Youthdigital.com offers online tech courses that teach kids ages eight to fourteen how to code, design, develop, and animate.

GIVE THE CODE A TRY

After the code is written in the text editor and saved, it has to be compiled so the computer can read it. To do this, the user types the command: *javac HelloWorld.java*. If all goes right, the compiler generates bytecode in a HelloWorld.class file. One of the great things about the Java compiler is that it will tell the user if there are mistakes, including which line or lines of code are wrong.

To see your program in action, you must then type "java HelloWorld" in the command line. Then the text "Hello, World!" should pop up on the screen. The command line on any computer is the powerful, controlling entryway. Be careful what commands you execute via the command line—punch in the wrong orders and you can wind up erasing all your data. If you have not been

```java
if (min > max) {
    throw new IllegalArgumentException("min > max: m
}

return IntStream.rangeClosed(min, max)
        .mapToObj(FizzBuzz::fizzBuzzify);


private static String fizzBuzzify(final int value) {
    StringBuilder stringBuilder = new StringBuilder();
    boolean toDefault = true;
    if (value % 3 == 0) {
        stringBuilder.append("Fizz");
        toDefault = false;
    }

    % 5 == 0) {
                        "Buzz");
```

>> Java, like every other programming language, needs to be written very exactly. A single error in the code can cause the entire program to shut down.

programming, you might not know where the command line is. For example, Apple's Mac OS systems store the command line in a program called Terminal, which can be found in the Utilities folder in Applications. Computer science teacher David Baumgold says that Windows has its own command line, but it is difficult to use. He recommends installing a free and easy command line program called Babun.

PLAY AND EXPERIMENT

After completing a simple exercise such as this, a novice programmer may want to think of easy projects that are of personal interest. Pursing a goal you choose can be more motivating when it comes to learning. You may want to make an image of a horse move from one side of the screen to the other. You might create a random insult generator, which might spew out a phrase like "Thou reeky puke-stockinged maggot-pie!" You might want to explore making a simple two-dimensional game. The key to learning is trying some projects and seeing how they work.

JAVA IN ACTION

C oders are the kings and queens of taking big problems and breaking them down into simple steps. Coding makes the world easier because it automates work—but it takes the hands-on labor of writing the code to get results that will make others' lives easier. Like any skill, the more programming someone practices, the easier it gets. Seeing the results of coding in action can take some time. Programs often do not work on the first pass, so coders need the patience to go back in and try again. They need to look over lines of code to make sure everything is right. It requires a lot of precise checking of detail—that is why coders follow the old carpentry proverb "measure twice, cut once."

Common complaints about coding are that it can be frustrating, tedious, and boring. Some coding jobs involve a lot of cutting and pasting of preexisting code to get the job done. This can make the job easier, but sometimes it takes away from the creativity of the process. To keep coding interesting, programmers take on projects and challenges that interest them. Coding gives one

>> Learning coding, especially for an absolute beginner, can sometimes be extremely difficult. It is easy to get frustrated, but there is always light at the end of the programming tunnel.

the potential to make something original. To get inspired about learning Java or another program, picking a project that is fun and of personal interest helps.

MOTIVATION FROM *MINECRAFT*

A fun way to get into programming is through computer games, and *Minecraft* is not only one of the most popular games in the world, it also provides the tools to understand coding. With more than 122 million copies sold and 55 million users every month, *Minecraft* has become a worldwide phenomenon.

The Swedish video game programmer Markus "Notch" Persson started *Minecraft* as a hobby project. Although he never finished

>> Markus "Notch" Persson exploded onto the scene in 2009 with the release of *Minecraft*, which has become one of the most popular games of all time.

high school, Persson loved building with Legos, and he taught himself to code starting at age seven when his father brought home a Commodore computer. By age eight, he had written his first program. In 2009, his passions for Legos, games, and programming came together when he made the first version of *Minecraft*. Along with his creative partner Jakob Porsér, Persson started the company Mojang (Swedish for "gadget") that year to further develop and sell *Minecraft* and other games.

Minecraft was practically an instant success, selling about twenty thousand downloads in its first year—and often that many every day in its second year. In September 2012, Persson sold Mojang to Microsoft for $2.5 billion.

Minecraft is known as a sandbox game. It provides an infinite environment in which players can wander and change a virtual world at will, building structures with cubes. Characters in the game destroy blocks and replace blocks in a world filled with dirt, trees, water, clouds, lava, mountains, and more. Minecrafters can go online and interact with others in a multiplayer version. Sheep, pigs, cows, zombies, creepers, skeletons, boats, rails, and snow were added as the game developed.

To make blocks, tools, and materials, *Minecraft* supplies a vast inventory of items and a crafting grid. *Minecraft* developers created redstone, which allowed users to make circuitry. In this virtual universe, redstone is basically a means to carry "electricity," and it can be shaped and set up to make all sorts of inventions, from lamps and clocks to computers and factories. The game continues to add dynamic features, such as platforms that raise or lower on pistons.

JOIN THE MOD SQUAD

Programming comes into play here with a feature called mods, short for "modifications." Because *Minecraft* was written in Java, Java coding unlocks the world of customized mod making. *Minecraft* gives players the ability to change qualities of characters, objects, and landscapes. With Java, the skins—or the images that determine what a character looks like in the game—can be changed. A mod can add new characters to the game, alter the look and feel of the open world, or make it easy to build new structures.

David Dodge, the founder of CodaKid Online Kids Coding Academy, says that fundamentals of coding for *Minecraft* are easy to learn with drag-and-drop visual block tools. These tools demonstrate event-driven programming, which is written to respond to actions generated by the user or the system. In 2016, Microsoft and Code.org introduced a drag-and-drop platform for *Minecraft*. These code blocks may contain if-then statements (conditionals), loops, sequencing, arrays, variables, or other instructions. The drag-and-drop technique is a great first step into coding. Although it does not involve the syntax of coding, it visually shows how coding instructions fit together like a puzzle to bring a function to life.

With basic principles mastered, newbies can kick it up a notch and work with the actual Java language. On Codakid.com, David Dodge says that anyone can use Java to create a Thunder Hammer that shoots lightning, make a custom LavaBomb, or design other items of his or her own invention. The programmer brings his or her own creative vision to life. Once the code is executed in the game, the reward is instant. Users can have great fun seeing their own coded work in action in their favorite game.

To create a *Minecraft* mod, an integrated development environment (IDE) can help. This is a software application that provides a graphical user interface (GUI) that streamlines the work and helps debug software. One common IDE that happens to be great for Java mods is called Eclipse. Another tool for modding is an application programming interface (API). Popular modding APIs, such as Bukkit or Hmod, provide an interface that easily communicates with *Minecraft*. A source code editor such Notepad++ can ease the process of editing source code.

>>JAVA JIVE: LEARNING THE LINGO OF PROGRAMMING

As a person learns the ropes of programming, some common phrases are used to describe different elements. Here are a few terms that should help the beginner become more fluent in the language of coding.

Array: An array is a collection, group, or list of data or variables. It could be a list of names, for example. An array could be described as a variable that holds multiple pieces of data. Once the data is stored in an array, it can be retrieved by referring to the variable name and the key (or compartment name). A search engine may use an array to store websites found when a user does a search.

Class: A class is the code that is the blueprint for the object and describes its contents. The class describes data fields and defines operations called methods.

Conditionals: These are "if-then" constructs in codes that tell the computer if something is true, then do something. For example, if a bank account goes under $100, code may then issue a statement: "Insufficient funds."

Loop: A loop is a repeating piece of code that carries out a main task.

Scripting: Scripting is a specific type of coding written in a specific scripting language. All scripting is coding, but not all coding is scripting. Scripting languages do not need to be compiled—they are interpreted. For example, normally, a Java program needs to be compiled before running, whereas, normally, a scripting language like JavaScript or PHP does not require compilation.

Method: A method is an operation or procedure defined in a data field.

Sequencing: This is the arranging of an action or event so that it leads to the next ordered action in a predetermined order.

Variables: These are values that can change depending on the program. They can be created, edited, or deleted as much as needed.

EXPLORING THE WORLD OF APPS

Web applications cover a wide range of functions. They can gather input through online forms, tally voting polls, take product orders, book airline flights, or let a user log in. People can now go online to buy clothes, do their banking, or participate in discussions—all because of web apps. Users around the world can access the applications on their computer browser—so millions of people can actually be using one app at the same time.

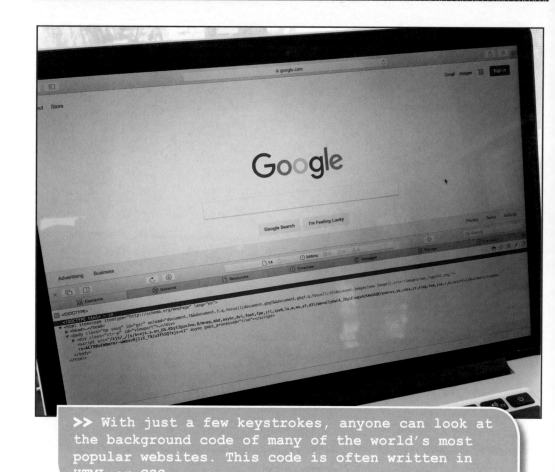

>> With just a few keystrokes, anyone can look at the background code of many of the world's most popular websites. This code is often written in HTML or CSS.

On the client side (seen by common users), websites may be constructed with markup or scripting languages, such as HTML (Hypertext Markup Language), CSS (Cascading Style Sheets), or JavaScript. Java is used for apps as well but often on the server side. For example, Java servlets are server programs that typically respond to requests from website users, most commonly an HTTP (hypertext transfer protocol) request. Java has built a reputation for doing well with large web applications that communicate with a number of other systems, such as those used by banks and insurance companies.

Java has grown to become the essential language for building programs that run on Android smartphones. Google chose to use Java as the programming language for its massively popular Android mobile operating system. Even the server-side functions of Gmail are run by Java and C++. In 2006, Google offered a Java-based application of Gmail for mobile phones. Apps let anyone do a broad range of activities via a mobile device, from playing online games to chatting with people around the world to viewing 3D images. Although Android has consistently relied on Java-based apps, Oracle has filed lawsuits against Google, claiming that Android infringes on its patents—while Google claims it legally incorporates Java technology under fair-use laws.

CHAPTER 4

CAREERS IN CODING

In May 2017, EdX—a massive online provider of university-level courses—named Java one of the three most lucrative programming skills you can learn online for free (along with SQL and C). The company spotlighted Java for opening the door to outstanding opportunities that often pay more than $100,000 a year. Numbers from the Bureau of Labor Statistics (BLS) show that the median pay for computer programmers was $79,840 a year in 2016. The TIOBE Index, which is a measure of the popularity of programming languages, ranked Java as number one in February 2018—meaning there are far more employment opportunities for those who know Java than any other language.

A vast range of employment options are available to the Java master. A Java software developer, for example, comes up with applications and software, often working together with web developers and software engineers to integrate Java into different business systems. The applications might be for mobile devices or tablets or could run on computers. All types of businesses and organizations use Java software.

DEVELOPERS AND PROGRAMMERS

Java coders might be working on word processing software, web browser tools, games, or media players, such as iTunes. Software development is often a very creative job because it requires coming up with new ideas. Typically, developers are involved in every step of a product, from its conception to its introduction to the world. Along the way, they are testing and analyzing the product, checking it for any potential problems. If there are any troubles, developers need to find a fix. They need to ensure they have the best quality product and that the program is user friendly. Also, developers may put together documents detailing the product so others understand all the details about it. Developers present the big picture about software structure and how it will operate with other programs. In many cases, they produce diagrams and flowcharts that explain how to write the code, but then they pass off the actual code writing to programmers.

Programmers can have a less creative job compared to the developers. They execute the plan presented by the developer, spending their days writing tons of code. They also debug (test and fix mistakes) and collect information into libraries that may be used later and make future code writing easier. Programmers can have different specialties. Game programmers write code that drives the graphics of computer games. Web programmers build the websites and applications that live with them. They may combine Java-based programs with pages built in HTML, the basic web development language. Web design brings together many skills, including computer programming and graphic design. The site creators know how to incorporate animation, video, audio, and interactive features.

Although designers and programmers are very much in demand in the technology-driven world, the US Bureau of Labor Statistics predicts that jobs for computer programmers will decline by 8 percent between 2014 and 2024. Part of the reason for this is that companies are hiring more affordable programmers from outside the United States.

EDUCATIONAL PATHWAYS

If programming and software development turns out to be a field you want to pursue as a career, you will want to move beyond online tutorials. Many major employers hire only those who have a degree in computer science, information systems, mathematics, or a closely related field. The coursework might cover data structures, computer architecture, database management, statistics, and technical writing. These are all important skills for any programmer using any language.

While the standard route to success in computer programming is through a college degree, a person who can demonstrate experience and a mastery of Java coding can still land a terrific position. Oracle has its own "university" that provides online courses and certification. Passing an official proficiency exam raises the value of a job candidate. As many programmers and developers will testify, the educational process never ends. The world of coding continually changes, so professionals need to keep up with all the latest advances. Even senior programmers have to master new features as they are introduced. If you enter this as a career, be ready to enjoy a lifetime of learning.

>>INTERNSHIPS GIVE A REAL-WORLD VIEW

There's nothing like working a real-world job to see what a career is really like. Those earning a college degree in computer science can often take advantage of internship opportunities through their school. Internships give students real-world work experience while also earning course credit. Most major companies offer computer science–related internships programs. Wal-Mart has one related to its online sales. Chevron seeks interns to assist on its applications, database management, and business analysis tools. Apple, General Electric, Hewlett-Packard, Verizon, IBM,

(continued on the next page)

>> Dozens of massive corporations, including Verizon, offer competitive internship programs for young computer scientists who have a strong background in coding with popular languages, such as Java.

(continued from the previous page)

Boeing, Microsoft, Target, Comcast, Dow Chemical, Dell, Humana, Oracle, Time Warner, and thousands of other corporations have technology internships.

Students may research problems and help develop and implement solutions. Working with skilled professionals, students master technological terms and understand the most current challenges in the tech world. Internships also often lead to invaluable job contacts. It is both a chance to build a résumé by taking on new responsibilities and a chance to build a network of professional connections that may turn into sources for recommendations or even full-time employment.

AN ENGLISH MAJOR MASTERS JAVA

Not all Java and coding experts start out with a background in computer science. Jonathan Feinberg is a senior software engineer at Google, where he works on code that powers a drawing engine, a tool that lets other software engineers add drawing features to their Android, iOS (an operating system used on Apple's mobile devices), and web applications. He writes the code in Java as well as C++, Objective-C, and JavaScript.

Although he grew up with a love for computer programming, that was not his first path as he entered college. While many of his colleagues have degrees in computer science, Feinberg has a bachelor's degree in English and American literature. Still, if someone is interested in a programming career, he recommends studying computer science or software engineering, and in the twenty-first century, it is good to know Java, C++, or Python.

Feinberg used Java to create Wordle, which is a toy for generating "word clouds" from text provided by the user. He has contributed to Processing (processing.org), a flexible software sketchbook and a language for learning how to code within the context of the visual arts. Feinberg has mainly worked on Processing's initial support for Android programming and Python Mode, which lets users create Processing sketches using the Python programming language (Python Mode itself, however, is written in Java).

He learned Java mostly by reading the first edition of *The Java Programming Language* and then coming up with fun little projects to challenge himself. He wrote a solitaire program and many other small programs to make animations.

For Feinberg's uses, Java offers the best toolkit for writing programs that provide interactive computer graphics. "The Java 2D API, as it's called, is still my favorite graphics toolkit—the one I most readily 'think in' when exploring or designing graphical programs," he says.

Java is also good for avoiding coding errors. He says that there are entire classes of bugs (programming errors) that simply cannot happen in Java because the language makes them impossible. "Those sorts of bugs are the cause of many crashes in C and C++ programs," he says, adding that Java's handling of errors is why many corporations (including Google) choose the language for certain large-scale software projects.

As far as disadvantages are concerned, Feinberg points to Java's reputation for being verbose. "It takes a lot of typing to express simple ideas," he says. "This can be frustrating, and lead to code that's boring to read. It can be a bit like having to write a novel by filling in tax forms."

AN APTITUDE FOR APPS

As a senior software engineer at Scientific Games Interactive, Will Rieder maintains and extends mobile social casino gaming apps by adding new features and troubleshooting existing ones. Two of their popular games are *Rainbow Riches* and *Spartacus Gladiator of Rome*. Although the majority of the company's code base is in C# or flash/actionScript, they use Java as a "glue" to interface with the Android hardware.

Rieder got interested in programming at age eleven when his advanced math class took a field trip to a local university computer lab. He found he loved the problem-solving aspect of programming—whether it involved playing a puzzle game or finding the best way to code a puzzle game. He says that the process requires him to ask, "How do I get from A to B? Is there a more efficient pathway between the two points?"

He picked up Java by using it to develop Android applications, and he says that right now there are a lot of opportunities for young people who know Java and other programming languages.

CHAPTER 5

POWERING TODAY'S TECHNOLOGY

As a computer language that is constantly evolving and still being developed to this day, Java remains cutting edge. The language regularly gets updates and new versions. The online Java community numbers in the millions, and users have assembled a large number of open-source libraries and development tools available to make programming challenges easier.

In an interview with Pearson Frank, a recruitment agency specializing in Java jobs, Jessica Kerr, a developer at software development company Atomist and a panelist on the podcast *Greater Than Code*, said that the world is moving faster and faster, and there is an increased need for automation. Because Java is practical and versatile, she sees it continuing to play a vital role in the future of technology.

STRENGTHENING APPS

In recent years, app development for mobile devices has grown substantially as consumers have become more attached to these gadgets than ever. The official language for Android app development is Java. In 2014, mobile internet usage surpassed desktop use. There is no doubt that the app business is enormous.

™

BANDAI NAMCO

Entertainment

>> Bandai Namco is responsible for developing and distributing some of the world's most profitable and popular mobile games, many of which are built and run on Java.

The app intelligence firm Sensor Tower calculated that global app revenue climbed 35 percent in 2017 to reach nearly $60 billion. Gaming apps sit at the top of the leaderboards. For example, Bandai Namco Entertainment's *Dragon Ball Z Dokkan Battle* brings in about $2 million per day in revenue. For those with a passion for game development, several websites have popped up to offer help, including Java-gaming.org and Lightweight Java Game Library (www.lwjgl.org).

For many people, apps like Facebook, Messenger, Google, Gmail, Instagram, Amazon, and Apple Music have been woven into their everyday lives. Music apps Pandora and Spotify, video streaming apps Netflix and Hulu, and other useful apps have soared in popularity as well. Many health-conscious consumers have turned to apps to track weight, calories, and exercise goals. In 2017, TechCrunch reported that although mobile app use has continued to grow, it may be slowing as the market has become flooded with an abundance of apps.

When it comes to app development, a programmer has to think about which platform his or her app will be designed for. Apple's iOS platform has been the leader, with Android not far behind. A 2017 report in Fuel.com said that 16 percent of Android app developers earn over $5,000 per month in revenue. A few teenage computer whiz kids have struck it rich with their app ideas. When Nick D'Aloisio was sixteen, he came up with Trimit, an app that condenses large amounts of text into shorter summaries. He wound up selling his idea to Yahoo! for $30 million.

BOOSTING BIG DATA

On a daily basis, businesses, governments, and other major organizations must deal with enormous amounts of data. They gather it, store it, keep track of it, and analyze it to make strategic business decisions. For programmers today, the challenge is keeping up with this ongoing tsunami of information. Antonio Regalado, senior editor for the *Technology Review*, said that only about .5 percent of all data is ever analyzed. Because Java is ready to use on desktops, mobile devices, and tablets—and offers vast libraries of code—the language can take on many of the tasks related to dealing with big data. By 2018, Hadoop had become a popular set of procedures and programs used to form the backbone of big data operations. Hadoop itself was developed in Java.

TO SPACE AND BEYOND

Java technology has taken steps into areas where no one has gone before. The National Aeronautics and Space Administration (NASA) uses Java in many projects, including its World Wind software development kit that provides a virtual 3D globe. Viewers can zoom in and out of various locations on Earth. Modern robotics engineering makes use of Java as well. An

>> NASA, just like countless other organizations, has made incredible pieces of technology using Java code.

award-winning self-driving car operates on the code. Dan Royer, who constructs and sells robots through his company, Marginally Clever, relies on Java. The language is also behind Makelangelo, an art robot that draws posters and murals. Combining the worlds of robotics and health care, Ali Lemus assembled a low-cost prosthetic hand. Lemus provides instructions on how to build the appendage using a 3D printer and Java code.

Thanks to Java technology, Doctor Online provides an interactive patient care service. In the world of show business, Industrial Light & Magic (ILM) has turned to Java for all sorts of effects. ILM has produced such effects as the squidlike face of Davy Jones in the Pirates of the Caribbean movie series and the photorealistic metal surfaces of Ironman's suit in many Marvel films.

The cloud is another cutting-edge area where Java has made its mark. Cloud computing is the practice of using a network of remote servers hosted on the internet to store, manage, and process data. Organizations and individuals access these computing services remotely. When someone stores data on or runs programs from his or her computer's hard drive, that is called local storage and computing—not cloud computing. Cloud computing services have become preferred by some as a more affordable option to owning and operating computers and networks. One example is Microsoft's Office Online. A user can tap into internet-only versions of Word, Excel, PowerPoint, and OneNote accessed via the internet without installing anything. They are cloud computing tools. Google Drive is a popular cloud form of file storage. Since Java can run anywhere, it has been well suited to cloud development.

>>OTHER TOP PROGRAMMING LANGUAGES

Java is often used along with other programming languages. Here are a few of the other widely used ones any beginner should learn about.

C: Widely used, C is a general-purpose language that was created in 1972. It is closely tied to the UNIX operating system.

C++: Able to run on a variety of platforms, such as Windows, Mac OS, and the various versions of UNIX, C++ has been one of the most popular languages for years. It was created in 1979 as a more extensive version of C.

C#: A hybrid of C and C++, C# was developed by Microsoft to compete with Java.

Objective-C: This is the primary programming language for writing software for OS X and iOS.

Python: A top-ranking language, this interactive, object-oriented programming language is free to use. It was named after the British comedy troupe Monty Python's Flying Circus. Many components of Google are written in Python, as are the games *Battlefield 2, Star Trek Bridge Commander*, and *Civilization 4.*

Ruby on Rails: Sometimes just called Rails, Ruby on Rails is an open-source web application framework that was built with the language Ruby by David Heinemeier Hansson. It incorporates Ruby with HTML, CSS, and JavaScript. Ruby is known among programmers for being an uncluttered language.

SQL: Structured Query Language is geared toward storing, manipulating, and querying data stored in databases.

EVERYTHING IS CONNECTED

In the rapidly changing technological world, a relatively new concept is the Internet of Things (IoT). This refers to the linking of all kinds of devices to the internet—kitchen appliances, driverless cars, heart monitors, and more. These electronic products connect via M2M, or machine to machine, communication.

Smart bike locks open and close via a special phone app— and if someone tries to tamper with a user's bike, his or her phone receives a text message. Devices now exist that track the freshness of milk and eggs in the fridge and send messages alerting consumers when foods have gone bad. The June oven and complementary June app lets users control cooking with their iPhone or iPad and monitor the food all via a live video stream. In theory, the technology inside devices also lets companies collect more data about their own products and their own internal systems. The research firm Gartner reported that an estimated 8.4 billion devices were connecting with the internet, sharing and collecting information, in 2017. One of the big concerns with the IoT, however, is security. Hackers have demonstrated how systems can be broken into to gain control of items like home security systems and computer-driven vehicles.

In an interview on Oracle.com, Vinicius Senger, founder of Globalcode, says that Java was born to do this kind of stuff. He says:

> Java has been all about providing corporate solutions, selling items on the Internet, and banking, but Java was initially designed as a programming language to connect things such as home appliances. Java is the best platform for the Internet of Things because it's flexible for computers of different sizes.

The same architectures, security, and communication protocols that Java applies to banks, retail enterprises, and internet businesses can be used on embedded devices. Java is the gateway into a brave new future of technology, programming, and convenience for everyone.

ANDROID A mobile operating system developed by Google that is based on an open-source operating system.

APPLETS Small applications that perform specific tasks.

APPLICATION PROGRAMMING INTERFACE (API) A set of routines, protocols, and tools for building software.

BUG A coding error or flaw in a computer program.

CLIENT SIDE/FRONT END Refers to actions that take place on a user's computer.

COMPILER Software that translates statements written in a programming language into machine language that a computer can understand.

COMPUTER ARCHITECTURE How a computer system is organized and structured.

DATABASE MANAGEMENT The organization and maintenance of information collected in a computer program.

DEBUG To find and fix errors in software or hardware.

EMBEDDED Describing a computer system with a dedicated function within a larger mechanical or electrical system.

GRAPHICAL USER INTERFACE (GUI) Often pronounced "gooey," GUI is basically the visual components that let a person use and interact with a computer. They are designed with visual elements that make the computer easier to use. Microsoft Windows and Apple Mac interfaces all use a "desktop" screen where icons are displayed.

INTEGRATED DEVELOPMENT ENVIRONMENT (IDE) A programming environment that streamlines the development and debugging of software and coding.

IOS A mobile operating system created and developed by Apple Inc.

MACHINE CODE An elemental language that a computer's central processing unit understands.

MOD Short for "modification," an alteration that changes some aspect of a video game.

PARADIGM A style or way of programming.

PROCEDURAL LANGUAGE A type of programming language that relies on a series of well-constructed steps and procedures.

PROTOCOL A set of rules or procedures for transmitting data between electronic devices.

SERVER SIDE/BACK END Refers to a computer that processes requests and delivers information to another computer over the internet or a local network.

SOFTWARE Programs used to operate computers.

SOURCE CODE Instructions written in a computer programming language.

SYNTAX A set of rules that specify how a computer language must be written.

TECHNICAL WRITING Easy-to-understand instructions, often used for products related to computer hardware and software, engineering, chemistry, aeronautics, robotics, finance, medicine, consumer electronics, and biotechnology.

TRANSISTOR A mechanism that controls current or voltage flow and acts as a switch or gate for electronic signals.

FOR MORE INFORMATION

Canada Learning Code
129 Spadina Avenue
Toronto, ON M5V 2L3
Canada
(647) 715-4555
Website: http://canadalearningcode.ca
Email: info@canadalearningcode.ca
Facebook: @canadalearningcode
Twitter and Instagram: @learningcode
This organization has a mission to provide digital skills to all
    Canadians—particularly women, girls, people with
    disabilities, indigenous youth, and newcomers.

Canadian Advanced Technology Alliance (CATA)
207 Bank Street, Suite 416
Ottawa, ON K2P 2N2
Canada
(613) 236-6550
Website: http://www.cata.ca
Email: info@cata.ca
Facebook: @CATAAllianceCEO
Twitter: @CATAAlliance
The largest high-tech association in Canada, CATA is a
    comprehensive resource of the latest high-tech news in
    Canada.

CIPS/Canada's Association of Information Technology
    Professionals
1375 Southdown Road

Unit 16 - Suite 802
Mississauga, ON L5J 2Z1
Canada
(905) 602-1370
Website: http://www.cips.ca
Email: info@cips.ca
Facebook: @CIPS.ca
Twitter: @cips
YouTube: @CIPSnational
This association offers networking opportunities, certification, and accreditation.

Code.org
1501 4th Avenue
Seattle, WA 98101
Website: https://code.org
Email: info@code.org
Facebook: @Code.org/
Twitter and Instagram: @codeorg
This nonprofit is dedicated to expanding access to computer science in schools and increasing participation by women and underrepresented minorities. Its vision is that every student in every school should have the opportunity to learn computer science.

CompTIA/Association of Information Technology Professionals (AITP)
3500 Lacey Road, Suite 100
Downers Grove, IL 60515

(866) 835-8020

Website: https://www.aitp.org

Facebook: @comptiaaitp

Twitter and YouTube: @comptia

This worldwide society of professionals in information technology offers career training, scholarships, news, and social networking opportunities.

National Association of Programmers

PO Box 529

Prairieville, LA 70769

Website: http://www.napusa.org

This group is dedicated to providing information and resources to help programmers, developers, consultants, and students in the computer industry.

TryComputing.org

501 Hoes Lane

Piscataway, NJ 08854-4141

(732) 981-0060

Website: http://www.trycomputing.org/inspire /computing-student-opportunities

Facebook: @TryEngineering.org

Twitter: @TryEngineering

This initiative from the Institute of Electrical and Electronics Engineers features competitions, events, internships, and research programs for young people. It also puts out information about career opportunities and colleges with computer programming courses.

FOR FURTHER READING

Bedell, Jane. *So, You Want to Be a Coder?* New York, NY: Alladin/Simon & Schuster, 2016.

Conrod, Philip. *Java For Kids: NetBeans 8 Programming Tutorial.* Seattle, WA: Kidware Software, 2015.

Garcia, Nadia Ameziane. *Java For Kids (and Grown-Ups): Learn to Code and Create Your Own Projects with Java 8.* North Charleston, SC: CreateSpace, 2017.

Guthals, Stephen Foster, and Lindsey Handley. *Modding Minecraft: Build Your Own Minecraft Mods!* (Dummies Junior). Hoboken, NJ: Wiley, 2015.

Hillman, Emilee. *Understanding Coding with Java* (Spotlight on Kids Can Code). New York, NY: PowerKids, 2017.

Horstmann, Cay S. *Core Java Volume I—Fundamentals.* 10th ed. Upper Saddle River, NJ: Prentice Hall, 2016.

McCue, Camille. *Coding for Kids for Dummies.* Hoboken, NJ: Wiley, 2014.

Thompson, R. Chandler. *Java Programming for Kids: Learn Java Step By Step and Build Your Own Interactive Calculator for Fun!* (Java for Beginners). North Charleston, SC: CreateSpace, 2014.

Vordeman, Carol. *Computer Coding for Kids.* New York, NY: DK Publishing, 2014.

Wainewright, Max. *How to Code: A Step-by-Step Guide to Computer Coding.* Asheville, NC: Sterling Children's Books, 2016.

Woodcock, Jon, and Kiki Prottsman. *Star Wars Coding Projects.* New York, NY: DK Publishing, 2017.

BIBLIOGRAPHY

Bedell, Jane. *So, You Want to Be a Coder?* New York, NY: Alladin/Simon & Schuster, 2016.

Beneke, Timothy. "A Perfect Match: Java and the Internet of Things." Oracle, June 2014. http://www.oracle.com /technetwork/articles/java/java-maker-iot-2214499.html.

Brain, Marshall. "How Java Works." How Stuff Works. Retrieved February 18, 2018. https://computer .howstuffworks.com/program2.htm.

Burd, Barry. "What Is a Java Virtual Machine?" Java for Dummies, March 20, 2017. http://www.dummies.com /programming/java/what-is-a-java-virtual-machine.

Carver, Cecily. "Things I Wish Someone Had Told Me When I Was Learning How to Code." FreeCodeCamp, November 22, 2013. https://medium.freecodecamp.org/things-i-wish -someone-had-told-me-when-i-was-learning -how-to-code-565fc9dcb329.

Charuza, Patrick. "How Much Money Can You Earn With an App?" Fueled, August 7, 2017. https://fueled.com/blog /much-money-can-earn-app.

Cleary, Annabel. "Top 5 Programming Languages for Beginners." CoderDojo, March 20, 2015. https://coderdojo .com/news/2015/03/20 /top-5-programming-languages-for-beginners.

Codeconquest. "How Coding Works." Retrieved February 18, 2018. http://www.codeconquest.com/what-is-coding /how-does-coding-work.

Dienhart, George. "List of Web Browsers That Support Java Applets." Techwalla. Retrieved February 18, 2018. https:// www.techwalla.com/articles/list-of-web-browsers-that -support-java-applets.

Griffith, Eric. "What Is Cloud Computing?" *PC Magazine*, May 3, 2016. https://www.pcmag.com /article2/0,2817,2372163,00.asp.

Heath, Nick. "Five highly-paid and in-demand programming languages to learn in 2018." TechRepublic, December 18, 2017. https://www.techrepublic.com/article /five-highly-paid-and-in-demand-programming-languages-to -learn-in-2018.

Kim, Larry. "10 Most Popular Programming Languages Today." *Inc.*, June 1, 2015. https://www.inc.com/larry-kim/10-most -popular-programming-languages-today.html.

Krill, Paul. "After a decade, open source Java is still controversial." InfoWorld, November 11, 2016. https://www .infoworld.com/article/3138505/java/open-source-java-at -10-big-benefits-but-detractors-remain.html.

Meehan, Frank. " My 8 year old taught himself to code Java. Here's how your kids can as well." Medium.com, June 22, 2015. https://medium.com/startup-study-group /my-8-year-old-taught-himself-to-code-java-here-s-how-yours -can-as-well-9b8f5ddcc56f.

Mueller, John Paul. "10 Surprisingly Interesting Ways to Earn a Living Using Java." New Relic, December 8, 2014. https:// blog.newrelic.com/2014/12/08/10-ways-java-money.

Oracle. "The History of Java Technology." Retrieved February 18, 2018. http://www.oracle.com/technetwork/java/javase /overview/javahistory-index-198355.html.

Prekash, Mayur. "The Importance of Java in Today's World." AllAboutWeb, July 7, 2016. http://www.allaboutweb.biz /importance-java-todays-world.

Sierra, Kathy. *Head First Java*. 2nd ed. Sebastopol, CA: O'Reilly Media, 2005.

Thumar, Chirag. "Current Trends in Java Technology." YourStory/MyStory, November 2017. https://yourstory.com/mystory/9c06c57017-current-trends-in-javas.

Woodie, Alex. "Which Programming Language Is Best for Big Data?" Datanami, February 12, 2018. https://www.datanami.com/2018/02/12/programming-language-best-big-data.

INDEX

ABOUT THE AUTHOR

Don Rauf is the author of numerous nonfiction books, including *Powering Up a Career in Internet Security, Computer Game Designer, Schwinn: The Best Present Ever, Killer Lipstick and Other Spy Gadgets,* and *American Inventions.* He lives in Seattle with his wife, Monique, and son, Leo.

PHOTO CREDITS

Cover Monkey Business Images/Shutterstock.com; cover, back cover, pp. 1, 4–5 (background) © iStockphoto.com/letoakin; p. 5 The AGE /Fairfax Media/Getty Images; p. 6 Sergiy Palamarchuk /Shutterstock.com; p. 9 Tero Vesalainen/Shutterstock.com; p. 10 (left) ibreakstock/Shutterstock.com, (right) ThomasDeco/Shutterstock.com; p. 13 David Maung/Bloomberg/Getty Images; p. 15 Anna Hoychuk /Shutterstock.com; p. 18 kr7ysztof/E+/Getty Images; p. 19 NicoElNino /Shutterstock.com; p. 21 Twinsterphoto/Shutterstock.com; p. 23 chaipanya/Shutterstock.com; p. 25 gOd4ather/Shutterstock.com; p. 27 Mehaniq/Shutterstock.com; p. 30 Antonio Guillem /Shutterstock.com; p. 31 Paul Hennessy/Polaris/Newscom; p. 36 Rosen Publishing; p. 41 Paul J. Richards/AFP/Getty Images; p. 46 Chesnot/Getty Images; p. 48 Tony Craddock/Shutterstock.com.

Design and Layout: Nicole Russo-Duca; Editor: Siyavush Saidian Photo Researcher: Nicole DiMella